D0712879

My First Pet

Rabbits

by Cari Meister

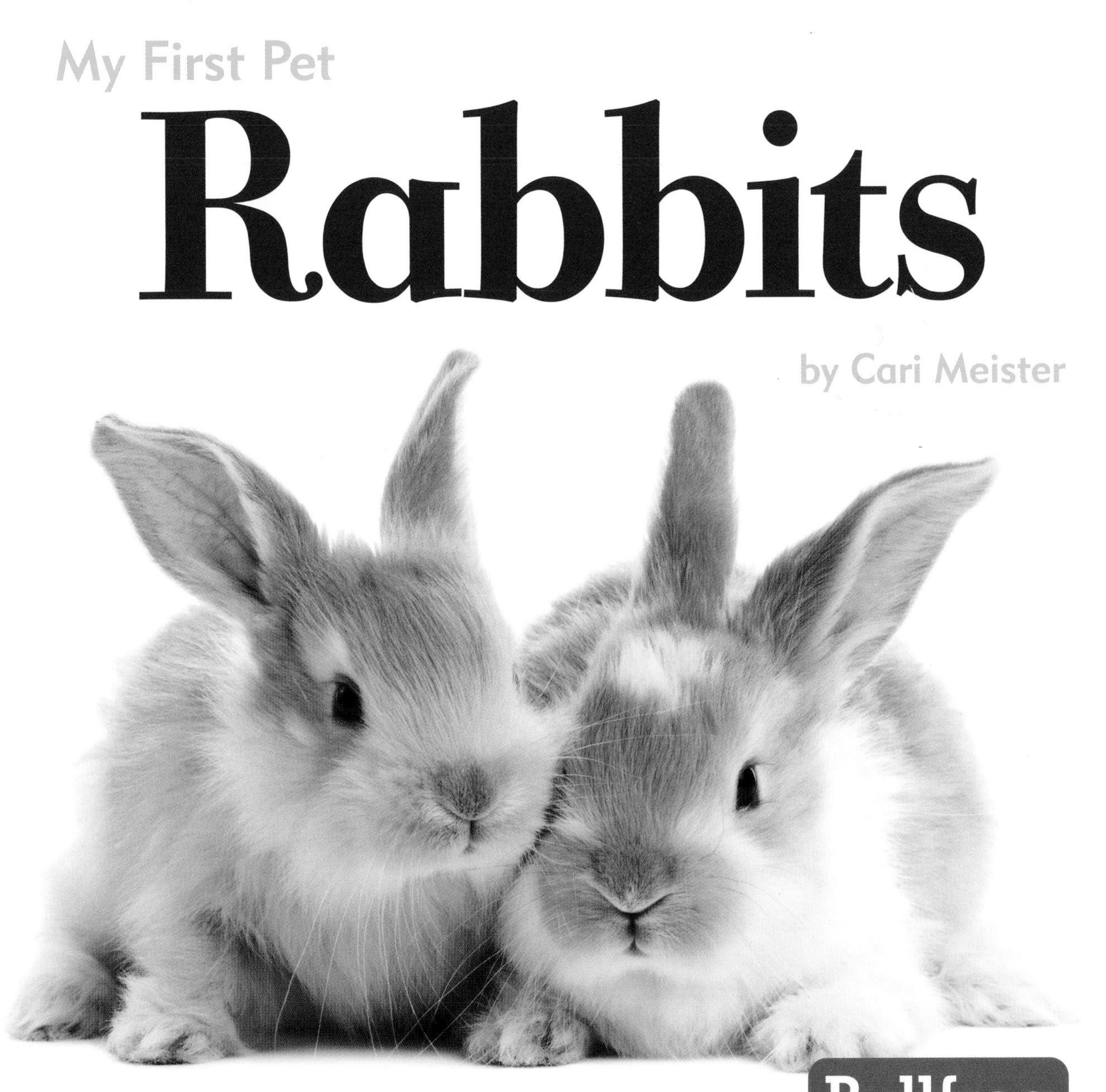

Bullfrog Books

Ideas for Parents and Teachers

Bullfrog Books let children practice reading informational text at the earliest reading levels. Repetition, familiar words, and photo labels support early readers.

Before Reading

- Ask the child to think about pet rabbits. Ask: What do you know about rabbits?
- Look at the picture glossary together. Read and discuss the words.

Read the Book

- "Walk" through the book and look at the photos. Let the child ask questions. Point out the photo labels.
- Read the book to the child, or have him or her read independently.

After Reading

- Prompt the child to think more. Ask: What do you need to take care of a rabbit? Would you like to own a rabbit?

Bullfrog Books are published by Jump!
5357 Penn Avenue South
Minneapolis, MN 55419
www.jumplibrary.com

Library of Congress Cataloging-in-Publication Data

Meister, Cari, author.
Rabbits / by Cari Meister.
pages cm. — (My first pet)
Summary: "This photo-illustrated book for early readers tells how to take care of a pet rabbit" — Provided by publisher.
Audience: Ages 5-8.
Audience: K to grade 3.
Includes bibliographical references and index.
ISBN 978-1-62031-125-7 (hardcover) —
ISBN 978-1-62496-192-2 (ebook) —
ISBN 978-1-62031-147-9 (paperback)
1. Rabbits — Juvenile literature. 2. Pets — Juvenile literature. I. Title.
QL737.L32M45 2015
636.932—dc23

2013045663

Series Editor: Rebecca Glaser
Series Designer: Ellen Huber
Book Designer: Anna Peterson
Photo Researcher: Casie Cook

Photo Credits: All photos by Shutterstock except: Marta Nardini/Getty, 5; Exactostock/SuperStock, 6; Superstock, 8; imagebroker.net/SuperStock, 10-11; Ableimages/SuperStock, 11; FLPA/SuperStock, 12-13; Juniors/SuperStock, 16; Bcarosio/iStock, 16-17; Lori Adamski Peek/Getty, 20-21; D. Hurst/Alamy, 22; Exactostock/SuperStock, 23; imagebroker.net/SuperStock, 23

Printed in the United States of America at Corporate Graphics, in North Mankato, Minnesota.
6-2014
10 9 8 7 6 5 4 3 2 1

Table of Contents

A New Pet

Zed wants a pet.

He wants a bunny!

The breeder has many rabbits.

Li picks a white bunny.

It has short hair.

hutch

What do rabbits need?

Katy makes a hutch for Fluffy.

It is big.

It keeps her safe.

water
bottle

Noah cleans Flower's hutch.
He takes out old shavings.
He puts in new ones.
He fills the water bottle.

Emily feeds Baxter.
He eats hay and vegetables.
He eats rabbit pellets.

pellets

Rabbits have big teeth.
They grow and grow.
Leo chews on a stick.
It keeps his teeth from getting too long.

teeth

Mike takes Bun out of his hutch.

He hides a carrot.

Bun hops. He sniffs. He digs. He finds it!

Rabbits are fun pets.

What Does a Rabbit Need?

chewing toy
Rabbits need something to chew.

water bottle
Rabbits need clean, fresh water every day.

Timothy hay
Rabbits eat hay every day. Timothy hay is the best kind of hay for rabbits.

Picture Glossary

breeder
A person who raises animals to sell.

pellets
A mix of crushed up food made into small chunks.

hutch
A large cage that a pet rabbit is kept in.

shavings
Bedding used for animals that can be made of wood or paper.

Index

To Learn More

Learning more is as easy as 1, 2, 3.

1) Go to www.factsurfer.com

2) Enter "pet rabbit" into the search box.

3) Click the "Surf" button to see a list of websites.

With factsurfer.com, finding more information is just a click away.